HUMANISTIC EDUCATION: Objectives and Assessment

A Report of the ASCD Working Group on Humanistic Education

Arthur W. Combs, Chairperson
David N. Aspy
Doris M. Brown
Morrel J. Clute
Laurabeth H. Hicks

Foreword by
Elizabeth S. Randolph

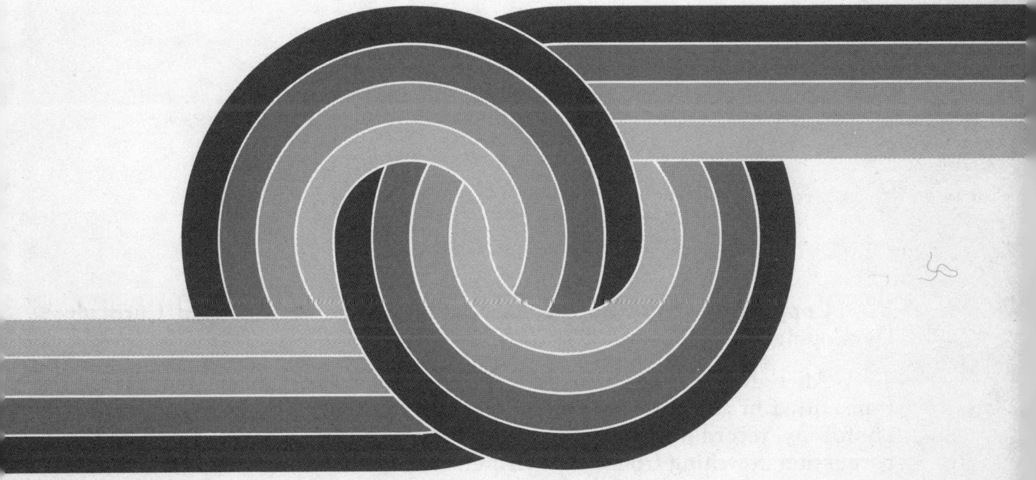

Association for Supervision and Curriculum Development
1701 K Street, N.W., Suite 1100, Washington, D. C. 20006

Stock number: 611-78136
Library of Congress Catalog Card Number: 78-57064
ISBN 0-87120-089-9

Contents

Acknowledgments

Final editing of the manuscript and publication of this booklet were the responsibility of Robert R. Leeper, Associate Director and Editor, ASCD publications. Additional editorial and production services were provided by Nancy Olson, Production Manager, with the assistance of Myra K. Taub, Teola T. Jones, Elsa Angell, and Patsy Connors. The cover design of this volume is by McMeans Graphics.

Foreword

Although the topic of Humanistic Education has often been discussed and debated in ASCD publications, there has never been a more appropriate time for a common sense guide for humanistic goals and objectives and for their assessment. Most educators are aware of the social, political, and economic phenomena that have created the demand for accountability in public education. The public has been especially insistent on the development of measurement instruments for competence in the basic skills. Many educators committed to the goal of humanizing education have been fearful that the accountability and "back to basics" movements could turn back the advances in humanistic education that have been made in the past decade.

This timely monograph prepared by task forces of ASCD's Working Group on Humanistic Education puts aside rhetoric. It recognizes that, for humanistic education to become a reality rather than a pie in the sky theory, it must be clearly defined, the goals must be stated, and assessment must be possible.

Humanistic Education: Objectives and Assessment provides educators and lay people a clearly stated readable text for beginning the task of humanizing schools. It offers no single solution but instead some very practical suggestions for individual districts to explore as they formulate their own plan.

Recognizing that humanistic education has been more honored than practiced, the introduction asks the question, "Why a Humanistic Movement?". Because technological advancements make determining all the basic skills our students will need in the future an impossibility, schools must provide education for a citizenry that can responsibly interact with one another and the environment in a fast changing world. If today's student is to become that kind of citizen, he or she must fully participate in the learning process and can be "taught at" no longer.

The body of this monograph is divided into three parts. The first presents a general definition and goals and objectives for humanistic education. Part II deals with assessment and research. The final section contains a versatile checklist for humanistic schools. Together, these three parts provide a compact yet comprehensive primer in humanistic education.

Humanistic education is defined in Part I by Morrel J. Clute. The general goals stated in this section are clearly compatible with those of parents and educators concerned with academic achievement. They go beyond the concern for basic education to the human foundation of education upon which any meaningful learning must rest. The task force recognizes that no one set of objectives would be useful for all local systems but offers instead a list of sample objectives that might be developed under each goal. It charges local systems with the task of developing appropriate objectives for their own needs.

Arthur W. Combs offers, in Part II, a look at some of the difficulties of assessing humanistic objectives. He gives the reasons why now, more than ever, such assessment is essential. The bonanza to educators is a list of a number of reliable ways that humanistic goals can be assessed. In this same section David Aspy and Laurabeth Hicks discuss some guidelines for research procedures, list examples of teacher behaviors and practices that can be used in writing objectives, and present a research model that is compatible with the goals of humanistic education.

Part III will be of use to any group interested in exploring humanistic education. Doris M. Brown not only offers a checklist for humanistic schools but also suggests a variety of ways to organize, to score, and to use the checklist.

This booklet should be included in any current professional collection. It will be of use to teacher trainers, curriculum planners, administrators, school boards, teachers, and parents. It will help bridge the gap between humanists and behaviorists. The most important contribution of *Humanistic Education: Objectives and Assessment* will be the giant step it takes in translating humanistic theory into practice in the school.

Elizabeth S. Randolph, *President, 1977-78*
Association for Supervision
and Curriculum Development

Preface

There have always been humanistic goals for education in America. The Humanist Movement is an effort to achieve a better balance in emphasis between humanistic goals and the more easily measured behavioral objectives. The hoped-for outcomes of all organized education are humane people who not only respect themselves, but also have the desire to treat other people with respect and dignity. If education is to place high priority on the development of humane people, it must utilize and expand those methods and practices that are known to facilitate positive growth and eliminate those administrative structures, policies, and teaching procedures that make the achievement of humanistic goals difficult.

Humanistic teachers do not advocate humanism simply because they want to be nice to everyone. They adopt humanistic approaches because they know that students learn better under such conditions. It is a better road to excellence, not only in human relationships, but in reading, writing, chemistry, geography, social studies, or any other traditional subject. The Humanist Movement is not fad or frill. It is an absolute necessity for our times. If it did not exist, we would have to invent it.

To provide further impetus for the humanist movement in education, ASCD's Working Group on Humanistic Education directed its studies toward four major needs:

1. A need for a clear definition of humanistic education which would help educators and laypersons toward a more common understanding of what is meant by the term.

2. A need to define some of the most significant humanistic objectives to provide more adequate bases for planning educational experiences. This, and the need for an appropriate definition of humanistic education

were assigned to a task force under the leadership of Morrel J. Clute.

3. The need for appropriate and workable techniques for the assessment of humanistic objectives. Arthur W. Combs provided a set of general considerations about assessment of humanistic goals and David N. Aspy and Laurabeth H. Hicks led a task force exploring ways to assess humanistic objectives for research.

4. The need for a simple device by which interested parents, teachers, citizens, and educators might judge the humaneness of their local schools. Responsibility for the development of such a Checklist for Humanistic Schools was assigned to Doris M. Brown.

The reports and recommendations of these task forces are the subject of this monograph.

David N. Aspy
Doris M. Brown
Morrel J. Clute
Laurabeth H. Hicks
Arthur W. Combs, Chairperson

Introduction

Why a Humanist Movement?

About a hundred and fifty years ago the people of America committed themselves to the idea of universal education, at least through the high school years. Since that time every list of objectives for our public schools, right down to the last White House Conference on Children and Youth in 1970, has always included humanistic objectives for education side by side with those having to do with acquiring skills, content, or subject matter. Among these objectives one always finds humanistic goals such as: worthy home membership, good citizenship, commitment to democratic ideals, self-esteem, a healthy mind in a healthy body, concern for other people, responsibility, creativity, intelligent behavior, lack of prejudice, preparation for change, effective use of leisure time, and many more. Despite these oft-stated goals, humanistic aspects of education have been more often honored in the breach than in practice.

Before we committed ourselves to universal public education, schools had a set curriculum and students were considered lucky to have an opportunity to attend. If they did not absorb what was taught, nobody worried much. They might even be thrown out of school as a waste of the teacher's time. The moment we made the decision to educate everyone, all that should have changed. In a system committed to educating everyone, the problem is no longer one of adjusting the student to the curriculum; the curriculum must be tailored to the needs of students. Now, a hundred and fifty years later, many schools are doggedly continuing the search for some magic formula by which it will be possible to ignore the individual nature of students and the qualities that make them human.

An educational system in these times must be humanistically oriented for at least four very important reasons:

1. *The basic change in human problems.* Since the dawn of history, a primary problem has been the control of environment—how to wrest from the physical world the means for food, clothing, shelter, and the protection of one's self and those one cared for. The advances of science and industrial know-how have now placed at our command the means to feed, clothe, and house an entire world, only to find ourselves faced with a new problem, the human one. We have created the most complex, interdependent society the world has ever known. Each of us is thoroughly dependent upon thousands of persons we have never seen or heard of for the provision of even the simplest necessities of life. We have become in truth "our brother's keeper." Side by side with this interdependence we have immensely increased the power for good or evil in the hands of individuals. A single terrorist can throw our world into chaos and every driver on the freeway has at his or her fingertips a powerful projectile capable of wreaking havoc and destruction.

The Humanist Movement came into being very largely in response to this fundamental change in human problems, such as ecology, starvation, overpopulation, conservation, atom bombs, and nuclear power. For solution, these problems require responsible citizens, persons of good will, *caring* persons willing and able to pull their full share in our complex society. The Humanist Movement is an expression of people everywhere seeking the defense of human dignity and the advancement of individual freedom to move toward personal fulfillment. One sees the fruits of this movement in such world-wide developments as the decline of colonialism, the rise of the have-not nations, the establishment of the world court, the United Nations, UNESCO, diplomatic attempts to forestall wars, the yearning of people everywhere for peace, economic pacts aimed at increasing distribution of goods and services, growth of popular government, the decline of dictatorships, the adoption of the concept of public education, increased freedom for women, the rise of labor, socialized medicine, the civil rights movement, and many more. In the United States the movement has found expression in the past 50 years in the practical elimination of child labor, in social security, medicare and medicaid, in research on physical and mental health, in equal rights legislation, and, most recently, in women's liberation.

The greatest problems facing all of us are essentially human ones. If education is to assume its responsibility to prepare young people to meet the challenges of the future, it must number humanistic objectives high among its priorities.

2. *The future can no longer be foreseen.* When public education began, the citizens assumed that schools would teach the specific skills people needed to deal with the future. That goal is now a pipe dream. Two things have done us in: the information explosion and the extraordinary rate of change in modern society. These two factors have made it impossible any longer to forecast what people will need to know even a few years ahead. Never again will education be able to offer a curriculum required for everyone. Attempts to establish educational objectives in precise behavioral terms are no longer enough. Indeed, preoccupation with such systems will practically assure education's failure in its responsibilities to prepare youth for the future. New goals for education must be holistic and humane. Prime objectives must be the development of intelligent behavior, the production of self-propelled, autonomous, creative, problem-solving, humane, caring citizens. Such objectives call for a humanistically-oriented educational system.

3. *New concepts of human personality.* For 50 years we have formulated our thinking about human beings and education from a static concept of human personality. We have defined psychology as the "study of behavior," and focused our attention on ways to control and direct behavior through the manipulation of stimuli or the consequents of behavior. We have regarded motivation not as a question of what people want or seek but as a matter of how to get people to do what others wish them to.

Humanism offers a more comprehensive view. It regards behavior only as symptom, the external manifestation of what is going on inside a human being. The humanist believes that effective understanding of persons requires not only the understanding of behavior but also of the nature of an individual's internal life. It holds that the primary causes of behavior lie in people's feelings, attitudes, beliefs, values, hopes, perceptions, and aspirations. These are the things that make us human. They are also, say the humanists, the fundamental dynamics of behavior.

For at least 50 years most educational practice has been based on behavioristic psychology. With the science of psychology redefining itself to include humanistic concepts of human functioning, education, too, must expand its sights to include such broader bases for theory and practice.

4. *Learning, itself, is a human function.* The process of learning always has two parts: (a) confrontation with new information or experience, and (b) the learner's personal discovery of the meaning of that experience. Throughout the history of American education we have been

preoccupied with the information aspect of learning. Teaching has focused primarily on the basic skills of reading, writing, and arithmetic and the acquisition of ever larger amounts of content and subject matter. One reason for this preoccupation is probably the fact that it is infinitely easier to deal with such matters. Providing information can be easily manipulated and controlled by the teacher. Because we can do it so well, there is always a temptation to do it more, in the belief that if a little is good, a lot must be very much better. Personal meaning, on the other hand, lies inside the learner and cannot be changed without active involvement of the student. Providing people with information can be done with or without the attention or cooperation of learners. What meaning the student makes of it is always a human affair, occurring inside the learner.

One of the most outstanding contributions of humanistic thought to our understanding of learning is its concern with the self-concept. The self-concept, we now know, is the most important aspect of any human interaction, a major determiner of every behavior. It is a vital determinant of intelligence, human adjustment, or success and self-realization in any aspect of life. It is learned from experience, and, once established, is often self-corroborative. What happens to the self in the course of schooling may be far more important than whatever else schools think they are teaching. Self-concept is a vital part of the learning process and truly effective education must be humanistically oriented toward student self-concepts.

Currently we are spending millions of dollars and millions of hours on behavioral objectives, performance-based criteria, input, output, feedback, perting, PPBS systems, and the application of computer-based technology to educational problems. One may even hear teaching referred to as "delivery systems"! It is true that managerial techniques sometimes work, particularly when they are applied to the teaching of basic skills which lend themselves to concrete, observable, and predictable behavioral outcomes. Unfortunately, greater efficiency in the teaching of subject matter is not our most pressing need. American education is suffering, not so much from a lack of efficiency as a lack of humanity.

The human qualities of students affect every aspect of learning and cannot be ignored with impunity. Learning is a human process and the laws of learning cannot be overlooked because they are inconvenient. Modern education has simply no choice. It must attend to the humanistic aspects of learning or risk its own defeat.

Research has supplied overwhelming evidence that humane people develop only when their growing experiences nurture feelings of worth and adequacy. There is also research evidence from 42 states and 7 foreign countries clearly showing that not only will achievement gains be significantly higher with humanistic teaching, but there will also be greater gains in intelligence measures.[1] We can no longer afford the inefficiencies of non-humanistic approaches.

[1] David N. Aspy and Flora Roebuck. *A Lever Long Enough.* Washington, D.C.: National Consortium for Humanistic Education, Catholic University, 1976.

PART I
Goals and Objectives

Humanistic Education: Goals and Objectives

Morrel J. Clute

A Definition and Goals of Humanistic Education

Humane schools give careful attention to the needs and purposes of the learner and utilize programs and practices designed to help each individual develop skills, attitudes, and understandings necessary for individual self-fulfillment. Humanistic schools work to free people so that they may make wise choices, utilize and choose from the options that are open to them, and become all that they potentially might become. The unique nature of all human beings and therefore the uniqueness of all human experience is valued and understood. All students do not bring with them the same background of experiences and do not all learn in the same way. This often makes it necessary to state educational goals in very general terms. Goals stated in general terms, however, are difficult to measure and this fact has impeded the extension of humanistic thought and practice into our public schools. As guides for action, more specific objectives are needed. To provide such a beginning, the Working Group suggests the following definition of humanistic education and a series of seven major goals through which it may be more explicitly approached: *Humanistic Education is a commitment to education and practice in which all facets of the teaching-learning process give major emphasis to the freedom, value, worth, dignity, and integrity of persons.*

Humanistic Education:

1. Accepts the learner's needs and purposes and develops experiences and programs around the unique potentials of the learner.

2. Facilitates self-actualization and strives to develop in all persons a sense of personal adequacy.

3. Fosters acquisition of basic skills necessary for living in a multicultured society, including academic, personal, interpersonal, communicative, and economic proficiency.

4. Personalizes educational decisions and practices. To this end it includes students in the processes of their own education via democratic involvement in all levels of implementation.

5. Recognizes the primacy of human feelings and utilizes personal values and perceptions as integral factors in educational processes.

6. Develops a learning climate which nurtures growth through learning environments perceived by all involved as challenging, understanding, supportive, exciting, and free from threat.

7. Develops in learners genuine concern and respect for the worth of others and skill in conflict resolution.

Humanistic Objectives

To accomplish the humanistic goals listed here, it is clear that much more specific objectives need to be developed as steps through which humanistic goals may be achieved. Because people are unique and local needs, conditions, schools, and classrooms differ, each school or classroom must develop objectives consistent with its own circumstances and goals. Some of these objectives will no doubt overlap with those of other people and places. Others will be unique, the products of special needs, persons, opportunities, and concerns. No one can successfully mandate humanistic objectives into being, but it is helpful to explore what research and authorities in the field have identified as practices and climates conducive to humanistic outcomes.

Accordingly, we have listed under each of the goals mentioned earlier some objectives suggested by research and experience as essential for humanistic schools and practice. The reader will note that many of the objectives listed under one goal apply to other goals as well.

Goal One: Humanistic Education accepts the learner's needs and purposes and develops experiences and programs around the unique potentials of the learner.

Sample Objectives:

Students demonstrate a willingness to attempt new learning experiences even when the experience involves the risk of failure.

Student learning styles are assessed, and instruction is planned accordingly.

Students choose curriculum content and methodology from a range of available options.

Students help to establish purposes and help to plan how these purposes will be achieved.

Genetic growth patterns are respected and used as a basis for teaching.

Subjects are taught when a child is ready rather than at a given age or grade.

Students are given time to browse, to paint, to muse, to dream, to think, to touch, to read, to love—to feel the quality of experience, its beauty and its ugliness.

Teachers facilitate students' attainment of students' personal goals by providing a wide variety of learning experiences.

Goal Two: Humanistic Education facilitates self-actualization and strives to develop in all persons a sense of personal adequacy.

Sample Objectives:

The teacher communicates clearly to children that learning is self-learning. Faith is demonstrated that all children want to learn and pupils show satisfaction as they become aware of their growth.

Each student experiences success in subject matter, human relationships, and the discovery of self as a person of worth and dignity.

Students will demonstrate a willingness to act upon freely chosen options.

Students will demonstrate ability to: identify possible choices in a given situation; describe possible consequences of each alternative; select an alternative; and justify their choice in terms of personal values.

Students see themselves as *able* to accomplish new learning experiences.

Students can act freely, knowing those around accept them as they are.

Students perceive themselves as growing each day.

Each child steadily increases personal feelings of dignity and adequacy.

Students find joy in their own self-development. They demonstrate willingness to permit other people to "be" and accept others as they find them.

Goal Three: Humanistic Education fosters acquisition of basic skills necessary for living in a multicultured society including academic, personal, interpersonal, communicative, and economic survival proficiencies.

Sample Objectives:

Students demonstrate skills in communication in its various forms.

Students demonstrate effective use of the processes of language, science, math.

Students demonstrate skills necessary for maintaining optimum physical and mental health.

Teachers help students understand the educational and social aspects of human sexuality.

Students have the experience and develop skills necessary for the creative use of leisure time.

Students work at developing skills necessary for participation in a democratic society.

Students demonstrate an interest in and a desire to develop skills which will enable them to live environmentally compatible life styles.

Students develop skills necessary for vocational and economic adequacy.

Goal Four: Humanistic Education personalizes educational decisions and practices. To this end it includes students in the processes of their own education via democratic involvement in all levels of implementation.

Sample Objectives:

Students demonstrate their ability to develop personal educational programs which involve: assessing needs and purposes, exploring educational options commensurate with identified needs and purposes, pursuing relevant options, constantly reassessing and evaluating progress to determine new needs and purposes.

Schools do not place unrealistic expectations on what may be explored. Teachers and students are free to look at whatever is needed to deal effectively with problems.

Teachers are inclined toward the use of decision-making at every level of school operation.

Evaluation is used as a diagnostic feedback tool to facilitate planning for future learning experiences rather than as a punitive measure.

There are no arbitrary standards for promotion, based on external standards too difficult for some and too easily attainable for others.

The school imposes no arbitrary methods of grouping and segregating students.

Children and youth are trusted to make "good" decisions in areas where they have experience and knowledge or, if they make faulty ones, are allowed to follow through. They are helped to explore the "errors" and take appropriate steps to correct them.

Curriculum decisions are made jointly by staff and students.

Students have free access to all information, test data, cumulative records, evaluations, and inventories necessary for realistic self-appraisal.

Goal Five: Humanistic Education recognizes the primacy of human feelings and utilizes personal values and perceptions as integral factors in educational processes.

Sample Objectives:

Teachers provide a climate which encourages full acceptance of feelings, of anger or sorrow or joy, to help children understand the emotional qualities of living.

Teachers use many open-ended questions to provide room for difference and the exploration of many answers.

Teachers exhibit faith that children can find answers satisfying both to themselves and others.

Teachers demonstrate a willingness to respond to students' needs and purposes by giving them priority over subject matter disciplines.

Evaluation procedures are open-ended to allow pupils to express their understanding and interpretation of information. Knowledge of facts is not enough.

Teachers attempt to know the reality of a child's environment, to understand how the child sees it, and what his or her perceptions are.

Evaluation is a shared process and includes more than academic achievement.

Goal Six: Humanistic Education strives to develop learning environments which are perceived by all involved as challenging, understanding, supportive, exciting, and free from threat.

Sample Objectives:

Students can make errors—or even do wrong—and not lose face thereby. Mistakes are viewed as indicators that learning is progressing.

Schools provide opportunities for children to have contact with several age groups.

Flexible grouping procedures across grade and age and ability lines are provided to help children to value the process as well as the achievement of learning and growing.

Children are free to express what they feel and seem secure in their knowledge that the teacher likes them as they are.

Students perceive the learning atmosphere as supportive and challenging.

Students and staff demonstrate respect for the dignity and worth of each individual.

Students and staff perceive *others* as *able* to accomplish new learning tasks.

Students demonstrate an awareness of cultural and ethnic differences and of the contributions made by diverse groups.

Students and staff demonstrate increasing ability to disagree without being disagreeable.

Goal Seven: Humanistic Education develops in learners genuine concern for the worth of others and skill in conflict resolution.

Sample Objectives:

The school establishes appropriate limits of responsibility, and freedom is shared by staff and students.

Responsibility for establishing and maintaining structure and defining goals is shared by staff and students.

Teachers provide settings where teachers and children may live in an atmosphere of self-trust.

Teachers have freedom to be themselves, to be human.

Teachers are treated as people of dignity and integrity. They are seen as trustworthy and responsible in all phases of school operation.

Teachers spend more time listening to children, allowing them to use the teacher and the group as a sounding board when ideas are explored. There is less teacher talk.

Students demonstrate ability to employ a variety of conflict resolution strategies.

PART II
Assessment and Research

Assessing Humanistic Objectives: Some General Considerations

Arthur W. Combs

A major deterrent to the broader adoption of humanistic goals and objectives is the lack of acceptable means for assessing them. This is especially true at the present time when the press for accountability demands clear-cut evidence of accomplishment from schools and teachers. Humanism, like the rest of education, must stand prepared to demonstrate its value when subjected to public scrutiny. Furthermore, since people tend to state objectives in terms which they know how to measure, the lack of humanistic assessment procedures results in preoccupation with behavioral objectives and neglect of humanistic ones. A prime example of this imbalance can be observed in the hundreds of millions of dollars poured into programs and research on behavioral objectives and the comparatively small amounts devoted to the exploration of humanistic goals.

Even if these pressing conditions did not exist, the search for means of assessing humanistic objectives is essential for three other reasons:

1. For the implementation of humanistic objectives
2. For the evaluation of teaching programs and practices
3. For the facilitation of research.

Special Problems in Humanistic Assessment

Three special problems complicate the development of assessment procedures for humanistic education:

1. Many humanistic objectives are holistic or general in character and do not lend themselves readily to precise behavioral measurement.

Objectives like good mental health, citizenship, responsibility, creativity, concern for others, and intelligent behavior are either so broad and comprehensive or so individual as to make behavioral measurement impractical or impossible. The outcomes of such objectives occur in response to innumerable situations and are expressed in so many thousands of ways as to preclude any hope of precise behavioral measurement.

Many humanistic objectives, like creativity, responsibility, and intelligence, are also expressed in unique, individual, one-time responses which cannot be predicted in advance. The very essence of creativity and intelligence, for example, lies in the student's ability to invent effective and appropriate responses "on the spot." If it were possible to define such responses in advance, they would not be creative or intelligent!

2. To find ways of assessing humanistic objectives effectively, it will be necessary to recognize at the outset that new goals may call for new kinds of assessment procedures. Techniques of assessment in behavioral terms have been around for a long time and almost everyone is familiar with them. Psychologists have been using and refining them for three or four generations. As a consequence they often provide us with data that are sharp, precise, and easily quantifiable. Observing the behavior of others is also a process which comes to us easily. We are accustomed to making such observations from our very earliest days. The methods of behavioral observation seem logical, precise, straightforward, and we feel quite comfortable with them.

Many approaches to the assessment of humanistic objectives are far less familiar and may seem crude and imprecise when compared to behavioral techniques. Such apparent lack of precision, however, should not dissuade us from the search for new procedures. At this stage of the game we should even *expect* that techniques may seem primitive or crude. In early stages of development most techniques are. Scientists tell us that the first atomic pile they built under Stagg Field at the University of Chicago was a very crude device compared to the modern nuclear generating plant. Similarly, the humanistic movement is barely 20 years old and its techniques at this stage are bound to be less precise than they will be when we have truly dedicated ourselves to developing them. Meantime, they are what we now have and what we must work with.

We need humanistic techniques precisely because behavioristic ones are not sufficient to assess humanistic objectives in adequate fashion. To reject the use of humanistic techniques because they do not meet the requirements of behavioral measurement leaves us in the ridiculous position of continuing to assess with greater and greater precision what we already know how to measure while humanistic objectives remain unassessed, or, worse still, are not even accepted as valuable goals for lack of devices to determine their achievement.

Proper assessment of humanistic objectives may require breaking loose from old assumptions to discover new means of evaluation. Where that is necessary, the challenge should be met forthrightly. Humanistic teachers need not apologize if their techniques of assessment seem less precise than critics demand. We are doing very well at this stage of the humanistic movement. We will do much better in the years to come. We need to remind ourselves that the Conestoga wagon was a crude transportation device, indeed, but it made possible the opening up of a new continent.

3. Many humanistic objectives have to do with the inner life of students. They are matters of feeling, attitudes, beliefs, values, likes, dislikes, loves, fears, hopes, and aspirations. These are the qualities that make people human. They also lie inside people and so are not open to simple external description or assessment. They do not lend themselves either to familiar techniques of paper and pencil testing or to precise behavioral measurement. Though internal characteristics like feelings, attitudes, and beliefs can seldom be accurately measured with traditional techniques, there are ways by which they may be assessed in highly dependable fashion. Some of these are described here.

The Acceptability of Assessment Procedures

Before examining humanistic approaches to assessment more closely, a general comment about reliability of techniques is called for. Scientists are familiar with the necessity for finding new measuring techniques whenever they confront new areas of exploration. The validity of measurement does not lie in the technique employed, but in the disciplined *way* in which techniques are employed, the usefulness of the data obtained, and whether the procedure for assessment meets accepted criteria of reliability.

Among the accepted tests for reliability developed by scientists in the physical sciences are the following:

1. Feelings of subjective certainty. Does the hypothesis seem reasonable and accurate to the possessor?

2. Is the hypothesis consistent with all the known facts? Does it fit? Does it provide an adequate explanation of all the data?

3. Will it stand the test of mental juggling? Will it ring true when

confronted intellectually and subjected to the impact of other concepts, explanations, or suppositions?

4. Will it predict? Using the concept to make predictions, will these predictions be borne out in fact?

5. Is the hypothesis acceptable to other workers, especially recognized experts? Have other persons come, preferably independently, to the same conclusions?

6. Is the concept internally consistent? Does the hypothesis stand up when various interpretations are made to confront one another? [2]

Such questions for determining acceptability in the physical sciences are equally applicable to the social sciences. Applied to the assessment of humanistic objectives, they provide guidelines for developing assessment procedures. With these criteria in mind, we can explore some possible approaches to the assessment of humanistic objectives.

Fruitful Approaches to Assessment of Humanistic Objectives

There are three important sources from which assessment techniques can be drawn:

1. Some techniques of behavioral measurement can be directly applied to humanistic questions.

2. Some traditional behavioral techniques can be modified in various ways.

3. It may be necessary to invent new ways of exploring humanistic objectives.

In the section to follow we have briefly described assessment approaches drawn from all three of these sources.

1. *Behavioral Approaches to Humanistic Assessment*

Many familiar techniques of behavioral measurement can be applied to the assessment of some humanistic objectives as well. Simple counting and statistical data can often shed light on humanistic questions. For example, the budget for broken windows, the absentee count, the frequency of inter-racial incidents, the number of disciplinary referrals to the principal's office, the numbers of volunteers for school activities, even the volume of litter swept up from the lunchroom floor may provide important information about the attainment of humanistic objec-

[2] G. Allport. *The Use of Personal Documents in Psychological Science.* Social Science Research Council Bulletin, 1942.

tives. Some pencil and paper techniques like tests of attitudes, values, interests, and the like can also provide important data. Appearing later in this monograph is the Humanistic School Checklist, prepared by Doris M. Brown and her task force, which includes many behavioral indicators of humanistically operating schools.

Many of the humanistic objectives listed in the previous section of this report also lend themselves to behavioral expression. A review of those objectives, while asking oneself the question, "What kind of measurable behaviors would be indicative of the achievement of this objective?," will often provide important clues to assessment.

2. *Inferential Techniques*

Many humanistic objectives have to do with student feelings, attitudes, beliefs, understandings, and perceptions of self and others. Few of these can be adequately assessed by behavioral techniques. They can, however, be approached through the use of inference.

People behave in terms of their perceptions and beliefs. By observing behavior carefully, then, it is often possible to infer the nature of perceptions behind the behavior. This technique, sometimes called "reading behavior backwards," is often used by psychologists to measure such aspects of a person's inner life as self-concept, values, and beliefs. It operates as follows: (a) Studying some sample of a person's behavior; (b) making an inference about the feeling which produced the behavior; then (c) testing the accuracy of inference against further observations. In such fashion, over a period of time, it is possible to arrive at highly accurate understandings of a person's typical ways of perceiving himself/herself and the world. As a matter of fact, this is what all of us do with regard to people who are important to us. We are keenly aware, for example, of the attitudes and beliefs of our husbands or wives, our lovers, bosses, supervisors, or persons in position to add to or subtract from our own feelings of fulfillment or success. We do it so automatically that we are often able to predict the behavior of significant others with a high degree of accuracy.

The capacity to make such inferences is often called empathy or the ability to place oneself "in another person's shoes." It is a prime requisite for professional workers in counseling, psychotherapy, social work, and good teaching. Everyone makes such inferences with regard to important people. Even little children do it with remarkable accuracy. If we can but redirect or reawaken the skills we already have for making inferences, people are always telling us what they are thinking and feeling by the ways they are behaving.

Unfortunately, as grown-ups we drop the use of inference for persons beneath us in the power structure. So we are insensitive to children, students, or persons outside our own circle of valued acquaintances. What is necessary for the use of inference in assessing humanistic objectives is thus not a matter of learning something new, but a question of applying a familiar process, with disciplined care, to students and teachers whose humanistic characteristics we wish to assess.

The use of behavioral, objective devices for assessment in education has been so common for so many years that many have come to believe these are the only truly scientifically approved techniques available for evaluation. As a consequence, many teachers and administrators feel uncomfortable with the use of inference for assessment. The use of inference, however, has a long and respectable history in physical science. From its very beginnings, physical science has utilized inference to deal with those matters that could not be directly observed. So astronomers infer the particular spot in space where a new star will appear. Similarly, no one has ever seen electricity or the smallest atomic particles, but scientists can infer their nature and behavior from observation of the "tracks" these forces leave. Without the use of inference science would be eternally tied to the immediate and palpable.

Inference is a necessity for dealing with events not immediately observable or when we need to project the future. It is also an acceptable technique for educators when used with proper care and discipline. Its use is an absolute necessity for dealing with such objectives as changes in the self-concept, feelings, attitudes, beliefs, understandings, values, and human hopes and aspirations. It is also a necessity whenever we attempt to forecast future behavior of students. It is, however, incumbent upon the user to understand the nature of inference and to use it with proper care and safeguards. We have already seen that the making of inferences is a common human activity. The ability to make highly accurate inferences can also be greatly improved with training and practice. To meet the requirements of disciplined use, education can also apply the tests of validity utilized in the physical sciences set forth in the previous section.

3. *Holistic Measures and the Use of Judgment*

We have already pointed out the inadequacy of purely behavioral measures for assessing holistic or highly individual objectives like good citizenship, intelligent behavior, pulling one's own weight, or creativity. To assess such outcomes of education at this stage of our sophistication will probably require the acceptance of human judgment. Again, our long preoccupation with behavioral techniques is likely to cause many people to feel uncomfortable with judgmental procedures and to question their acceptability for assessment. Human judgment is, of course, open to human error. In the absence of highly precise devices for measurement it is also very often the only usable tool we have. We cannot afford to bypass the assessment of humanistic objectives because the available means of assessment are less precise than we might like. To do so will only distort the thrust of education leaving us forever concentrating attention on what we already know how to do while that which we desperately need to do lies untouched, blocked off by our fear of making mistakes.

A major goal of education itself, is the improvement of human judgment. Human judgment can be made reliable and precise when subjected to disciplined use and checked against standard criteria for reliability already mentioned earlier. Judgments made by human beings can be subjected to tests of internal and external reliability, ability to predict, agreement with expert opinion, and the like. Just as the physical scientist calibrates his or her instruments before using them, the judgment making processes of human beings can also be refined and adjusted to give reliable data.

4. *Critical Indicators*

Frequently overlooked sources of data for assessing humanistic objectives are critical indicators. In any highly complex operation, what is really going on can often be observed with great clarity from some comparatively simple event. Psychologists, sociologists, counselors, politicians, to name but a few, are continuously tuned to such critical indicators as, for example, the turn of a phrase, over- or understatement, defensive postures, or even the loud noises made by what people never said. It does not take an expert to understand what really bothers a mother who cries in indignation, "My child is failing first grade! How can I face my friends?"

Critical indicators often have the capacity to tell us volumes about what is going on in a particular setting. For example, a little boy with serious behavioral and academic problems in a fifth grade was shifted to another teacher's classroom. Some six weeks later the author met him and asked how things were going. "Oh, fine," he said, "Ms. Hildebrand makes me feel all *smoooooth* inside!" This single eloquent expression is probably a more significant indicator of what is going on in Ms. Hildebrand's class than any amount of statistics, questionnaires, or behavioral observations. Sensitive people are continuously attuned to such expressions and appreciate their value as indicators of the state of affairs in all kinds of settings.

Because critical indicators are so deeply expressive of the personal, human qualities of situations and events, they are especially useful for the evaluation of humanistic objectives. They can also be used with telling effect to sell or defend humanistic practices. Workers in such fields as advertising, sales, politics, legal practice, and many others are keenly aware of the power a well chosen illustration or anecdote can provide to enlighten an audience, defend a position, or persuade a reluctant citizen. Humanistic educators need to appreciate the usefulness of critical indicators and learn to use them for the advancement of humanistic objectives.

Example: A junior high school in one of our great cities had long been plagued with a record of vandalism and destruction. Near the end of the fourth year of a new principal's tenure, the custodian requested permission to speak to the student body on the public address system. Permission was granted and the custodian spent five minutes telling the students what fine people he thought they were and how much he appreciated the splendid way they had helped him keep their building a pleasant place to live in!

Example: A visitor, seeing a small boy standing in the hall outside his classroom door, asked him what he was doing there. "I was bad," the little boy said, "I laughed."

5. *Case History Evidence*

Most of the devices for assessment familiar to teachers and administrators depend upon horizontal examinations of data, cross-sectional observations made at a particular point in time. Examples of such evaluative procedures are pencil and paper tests, standardized examinations of many kinds, observational records, and demographic data. Such observations are useful in the gathering of normative data or establishing the nature of a given status quo. The achievement of humanistic objectives, however, is often so highly personal and individualized as to defy description in such fashion. Similarly, the dynamics of events which did or did not impinge upon a person or produce a change in his or her behavior can rarely be observed at any one moment. Important information for the assessment of humanistic objectives, on the other hand, can often be obtained from evidence gleaned from longitudinal studies following a given subject over a more or less extended period of time. Such case history evidence has long been used in social work, psychology, psychiatry, and anthropology, and can be equally useful for educators seeking to explore the achievement of humanistic objectives.

What happens to individuals lies at the very heart of the humanistic movement and normative data are seldom sufficient to provide the richness of information required for the understanding of a unique case.

Proper assessment of humanistic goals may require a series of observations over considerable periods of time. A child's self-concept, for example, is a highly stable perceptual organization, modified very slowly as a consequence of numerous personal experiences. Other humanistic objectives like responsibility, concern for other people, intelligent behavior, and the like are also slowly changing dynamics in a student's character. Case histories attempting to follow a particular individual over a period of time can often shed important light on such slowly changing characteristics. They can also help us become aware of possible dynamics in the child's school experience related to such changes.

The gathering of case history data is, of course, time consuming, bulky, and ordinarily cannot be done on large numbers of persons. Such data can and probably should be used, however, with students whose needs are being inadequately met by regular procedures or about whom teachers and administrators have special concern. Case history data can also make important contributions to communication with parents and the general public or in selling or defending humanistic practices in schools.

Good examples of such uses of case history data can be found in special education. Educators in the field of exceptional education have long used such data to gain support for their programs. A single touching story about a handicapped child can often be more valuable for communicating the special needs of such children to school boards and legislatures than reams of statistical data. The technique can be equally useful for communicating the special needs of humanistic education.

6. *Professional Opinion*

One of the more unhappy effects of preoccupation with behavioral measures is the distrust it creates for professional opinion. Exclusive insistence upon objective behavioral data and derision of teacher opinion seriously affect the morale of teachers by undermining confidence in their own professional judgments. Such lack of confidence in turn contributes to the public stereotype of teachers as a wishy-washy, Caspar Milquetoast bunch whose opinions don't really amount to much. Contrast this with other professions like law, medicine, or psychology in which practitioners typically operate with high degrees of faith in their professional opinions and are supported by a public which accepts their pronouncements almost as though they were infallible. The opinions of trained professionals about students and education are equally deserving of respect.

We have already seen that expert opinion is acceptable as a valid source of data in science. In the current state of our ability to assess complex human characteristics and behavior, professional experience will often be one of the few, if not the only, means available for insight into many humanistic objectives. Most objective data only have validity when subjected to interpretation and refinement from professional judgment. The human organism has an immense capacity to absorb and assimilate millions of observations into useful conclusions. Subjected to reasonable criteria for reliability such conclusions can be of great value for assessing humanistic objectives. The five members of this working group have among us more than a hundred years of professional experience and none of us is about to set it summarily aside or substitute for it simplistic behavioral measures. Experienced professional judgment is a valuable source of data for assessing humanistic objectives and deserves an important place in any assessment program.

7. *Experiential Report*

One way to find out about the achievement of humanistic objectives is to consult the consumer. The goal of humanistic education is to produce changes in the feelings, attitudes, beliefs, understandings, and values resulting in more effective behavior in the future. The behaviors expressive of humanistic objectives, however, are so diverse, so individual, and so related to specific circumstances and conditions as to make behavioral measurement well nigh impossible. But the beliefs or perceptions which produce behavior are much more stable and influence so broad a spectrum of behaviors as to provide important clues about humanistic goals. One way of measuring these internal factors is through the process of inference discussed earlier in this section. One source of data for making such inferences is the student's own report of his or her experience. A student's personal description of beliefs and understandings, of what happened to him or her and what personal effects it had, can often be useful data for assessing humanistic objectives when used with proper safeguards.

A person's self report is, itself, a behavior produced by feelings, attitudes, beliefs, etc., and cannot be accepted on a one-to-one basis as a straightforward expression of what is going on inside the individual. The report of a person in response to the question, "How do you see yourself?," for example, cannot be taken at face value as an accurate indication of how things truly are. A great many factors will determine the accuracy of the report including: whether the person believes we have any right to ask the question, whether he or she consciously or unconsciously intends to deceive either himself or herself or the questioner, whether he or she has the necessary words to express the precise meaning, what he or she believes are the expected replies, how secure he or she feels in the relationship in which the question is asked, what use he or she believes is going to be made of the material, what impact he or she hopes to produce by the answers, and many more. Despite these possible sources of error, experiential reports can often be highly useful indicators of humanistic objectives when used with care and understanding of the technique.

Spontaneously offered experiential reports, especially, can often be highly revealing of humanistic data, especially when they occur in settings where the reporter feels secure and unthreatened. Even in fairly structured situations they may provide invaluable data if sufficient care is taken to create conditions encouraging uninhibited expression.

The foregoing areas are but a few of the general ones within which educators can seek assessment techniques for humanistic objectives. Some can be utilized at once with little further development. Others are areas so new or so little explored in educational circles that they require much experimenting to bring them into fullest possible usefulness. A major contribution to American education can be made by research that is designed, (a) to explore these areas of assessment, (b) to invent new techniques, and (c) to subject innovative techniques to rigorous tests in action. We hope educational organizations such as ASCD, foundations, or colleges of education will recognize the need and the promise of such research and embark upon suitable explorations. We hope, too, that public and private funding agencies will recognize the potential good such research can do for the advancement of education and the pressing need for knowledge in these areas. So much is currently being expended for research on behavioral objectives, it is time we devoted at least an equal effort to the exploration of humanistic objectives.

Research on Humanistic Objectives

David N. Aspy, Laurabeth H. Hicks

Humanistic educators must be accountable. They have a responsibility, like everyone else in education, to demonstrate that the goals they seek and the practices they employ truly result in demonstrable educational benefits. To do this they must devote a significant part of their efforts to research on humanistic objectives demonstrating, not only that humanistic objectives have been achieved, but also that the efforts expended in their achievement have not been at the expense of traditional goals. Better still, humanistic educators believe the achievement of humanistic objectives actually increases the likelihood that traditional objectives will also be attained. As a matter of fact, there is already evidence that this is true, but there is still a great need for more research on the effects of humanistic approaches. Many more serious efforts at research in this area are called for.

One of the major concerns for ASCD has been a search for investigative procedures that describe the effects of humane education. Often that quest has been agonizing and discouraging because the problems have yielded slowly. Fortunately, a few of the obstacles are being overcome, and we are devising effective procedures which support ASCD's prime tenet, namely, that humane schools are better than inhumane ones.

As investigative efforts have moved forward, one very important principle has become clear, that humanizing is a lifelong process. It simply does not occur quickly. Conversely, neither does dehumanizing happen overnight. From a research point of view, this means that *time* is a crucial dimension in research into humanistic education. The general rule is that the longer the time factor, the greater is the probability that the investigation will delineate the effect of constructive human relationships. The commonsense model which supports this position is that it takes at least 20 years to be a constructive parent for one's child. Parents have to "hang in there."

The realization that humane efforts must be evaluated on a longitudinal basis is somewhat discouraging to both investigators and implementers. All of us would like to discover the "instant cure" with its spontaneous results. Unfortunately, this flies in the face of both the research results and the obvious reality that human growth and development proceeds across time. There does not seem to be any shortcut across the time variable. Despite this difficulty, in the short time we have been doing humanistic research, we have already made sufficient progress to demonstrate that humanistic objectives can be effectively assessed for research purposes.

Hypotheses for Humanistic Research

Many of the assessment techniques discussed earlier for use in informal evaluations of humanistic outcomes can also be used for research on humanistic objectives. Testable research hypotheses can be found in great abundance in many humanistically-oriented publications. One of the best such sources is ASCD's 1962 Yearbook, *Perceiving, Behaving, Becoming: A New Focus for Education*, regarded by many as a classic contribution to humanistic education. In the belief that human self-fulfillment or actualization is the fundamental goal of all helping professions, including teaching, the committee invited each of four scholars, Carl Rogers, Abraham Maslow, Earl Kelley, and Arthur Combs to write a paper on the fully functioning, self-actualizing person. The yearbook committee then sought to translate these understandings into basic principles for educational thought and practice.

The result was a yearbook providing a kind of blueprint for humanizing education which sold more copies than any ASCD yearbook before or since and still remains a popular reference after more than 15 years. This "New Focus for Education" is full of principles about humane people and facilitative schools. In many instances, it also lists fairly specific practices and outcomes amenable to assessment in educational settings and easily translated into promising hypotheses for humanistic research. For example, in Chapter 14 fourteen signs of creative teaching and learning are listed as follows:

- Less teacher domination; more faith that children can find answers satisfying to themselves.
- Less teacher talk; more listening to children, allowing them to use the teacher and the group as a sounding board when ideas are explored.

- Less questioning for the right answer; more open-ended questions with room for difference and the exploration of many answers.

- Less destructive criticism; more teacher help which directs the child's attention back to his or her own feelings for clarification and understanding.

- Less emphasis on failure; more acceptance of mistakes—more feeling on the part of the child that when he or she makes a mistake it is done, accepted, and that's it. As one child said, "She doesn't rub salt in."

- Children's work is appreciated, but praise is not used to put words in the mouths of children.

- Goals are clearly defined; structure is understood and accepted by the group.

- Within appropriate limits, children are given responsibility and freedom to work. "For once a teacher told us we could do it ourselves and really meant it."

- Children are free to express what they feel and seem secure in their knowledge that the teacher likes them as they are.

- Ideas are explored; there is an honest respect for solid information, an attitude of "let's find out."

- There is a balance of common tasks and individual responsibility for specific tasks which are unique and not shared.

- The teacher communicates clearly to children that learning is self-learning. Faith is demonstrated that all children want to become and pupils show satisfaction as they become aware of their growth.

- Evaluation is a shared process and includes more than academic achievement.

- Motivation for learning is high and seems inner-directed; pupil activity seems to say, "I've got a job I want to do." [3]

As a demonstration of how such humanistic objectives can be translated into effective research hypotheses, Task Force Three of the Working Group on Humanistic Education, under the leadership of David Aspy and Laurabeth Hicks, used these fourteen signs of creative teaching to formulate evaluation procedures which would be applicable to a wide variety of educational settings. The evaluation procedures can be used by both individuals and groups, so that one person or several people can apply them. The *signs* and *assessment* procedures are presented in the following section.

[3] Arthur W. Combs, editor. *Perceiving, Behaving, Becoming: A New Focus for Education.* 1962 Yearbook. Washington, D.C.: Association for Supervision and Curriculum Development, 1962.

Signs of Creative Teaching and Assessment Procedures

Sign I: Less teacher domination; more faith that children can find answers satisfying to themselves.

Rationale—Domination lessens when teachers use fewer controlling behaviors. Student initiation increases when students are more satisfied with their classwork.

Assessment Procedure

1. *Describe* classroom interaction according to Flanders' Interaction Analysis. This can be done from (a) observation of on-going class, (b) audio recording of class, or (c) video recording of class.
2. *Tabulate* the amount of class time occurring in categories 5, 6, and 7 of Flanders' Interaction Analysis. These categories describe the direct or controlling behavior of the teacher.
3. *Tabulate* the number of responses in category 9 of Flanders' Interaction Analysis. This is the amount of class time used by student-initiated talk.

Evaluation Guidelines

a. As the amount of behavior in categories 5, 6, and 7 decreases, teacher domination is also lessening.
b. As the amount of behavior in category 9 increases, students' satisfaction with their answers is improving.

Sign II: Less teacher talk; more listening to children, allowing them to use the teacher and the group as a sounding board when ideas are explored.

Rationale—The less the teacher talks and the more students talk, the greater the possibility that both teachers and students are listening to students.

Assessment Procedure

1. *Describe* the classroom interaction using Flanders' Interaction Analysis.
2. *Tabulate* the total behavior in categories 1 through 7.
3. *Tabulate* the total behavior in categories 8 and 9.

Evaluation Guidelines

a. The less the behavior in categories 1 through 7, the less the amount of teacher talk.
b. The more the behavior in categories 8 and 9, the greater the amount of student talk.

Sign III: Less questioning for the right answers; more open-ended questions with room for difference and the exploration of many answers.

Rationale—The measurement of this sign is very straightforward. The greater the number of open-ended questions, the more the interaction is characteristic of creative teaching.

Assessment Procedure

1. *Tabulate* the number of open-ended (divergent) questions asked by the teacher during a classroom interaction.

Sign IV: Less destructive criticism; more teacher help which directs the child's attention back to his or her own feelings for clarification and understanding.

Rationale—The measurement of this sign is straightforward. The greater the rate of destructively critical remarks the higher the possibility that the student learns that there is something bad about him or her as a person.

Assessment Procedure

1. *Tabulate* the number of statements by the teacher which indicate to the student that he or she is deficient, for example, "You shouldn't feel that way" or "You should be able to do that."

2. *Complete* the ratio $\frac{\text{number of destructive criticisms}}{\text{time observed}} = ?$

Sign V: Less emphasis on failure; more acceptance of mistakes. More feeling on the part of the child that when he or she makes a mistake it is done, accepted, and that is it. As one child said, "She doesn't rub salt in."

Rationale—The larger (numerically) the ratio of "good try" to "bad try" answers, the greater the possibility that students will learn not to feel "put down" by their failures.

Assessment Procedure

1. *Tabulate* the number of teacher remarks to wrong answers which communicate "That's a good try. Now let's see if we can improve it some."

2. *Tabulate* the number of teacher responses to wrong answers which communicate either (a) "You're wrong and you should do better than that" or (b) "He/she missed that question. Who can tell him/her the right answer?"

3. *Calculate* the ratio $\frac{\text{Good try answers}}{\text{Bad try answers}} = ?$

Sign VI: Children's work is appreciated, but praise is not used to put words in the mouths of children.

Rationale—The larger (numerically) the ratio between the invitational and manipulative remarks by the teacher, the greater the possibility that the student will learn that he or she is appreciated but not manipulated.

Assessment Procedure

1. *Tabulate* the number of teacher responses which indicate "If you'd like, we'd appreciate your telling us about your project, pictures, etc." (invitation)

2. *Tabulate* the number of teacher responses which indicate "I'll say nice things about you if you do what I want." (manipulation)

3. *Calculate* the ratio $\frac{\text{Number of invitational remarks}}{\text{Number of manipulative remarks}} = ?$

Sign VII: Goals are clearly defined; structure is understood and accepted by the group.

Rationale—The greater the percentage of students who (a) know the goals of the class and (b) like them, the greater the possibility that the class is meaningful to them.

Assessment Procedure

1. *Ask* a specific number of the students to state the goals of the class activity.

2. *Ask* the students who know the goals whether or not they like them.

3. *Calculate* the percent of students who (a) know the goals of the class and (b) like the goals of the class.

Sign VIII: Within appropriate limits, children are given responsibility and freedom to work. "For once a teacher told us we could do it ourselves and really meant it."

Rationale—The larger (numerically) the ratio between the assisting and interfacing behaviors, the greater the possibility the student will learn that he/she does have responsibility and freedom to work.

Assessment Procedure

1. *Tabulate* the behaviors in which the teacher assists a student after being asked by the student. (assistance)

2. *Tabulate* the behaviors in which the teacher corrects or does a task for a student without being asked by the student. (interference)

3. *Calculate* the ratio $\frac{\text{Number of assisting behaviors}}{\text{Number of interfering behaviors}} = ?$

Sign IX: Children are free to express what they feel and seem secure in their knowledge that the teacher likes them as they are.

Rationale—A student indicates that his or her expressions of feeling are accepted when he or she expands on them as a result of the teacher's response to the original expression of feeling. It is important to identify the sequence of behaviors. Each triadic sequence (A-B-C) is scored as *one* behavioral incident. One piece of the sequence is not scored in this approach.

Assessment Procedure

1. *Tabulate* the number of behavior sequences which follow this pattern: (a) student expresses a feeling, (b) teacher responds to that feeling, (c) student expresses more feeling or clarifies his or her first expression.

Sign X: Ideas are explored; there is an honest respect for solid information, an attitude of "let's find out."

Rationale—The larger (numerically) the ratio between thinking and memory ratio, the greater the possibility that a student will learn that ideas are important in the classroom.

Assessment Procedure

1. *Tabulate* the student and teacher behaviors which are statements of problems to be solved.

2. *Tabulate* the student and teacher behaviors which are statements of solutions to problems.

3. *Tabulate* the student and teacher behaviors which are recall of information (memory) or requests for memory.

4. *Calculate* the ratio $\frac{\text{Number of thinking behaviors } (1 + 2)}{\text{Number of memory behaviors}} = ?$

Sign XI: There is a balance of common tasks and individual responsibility for specific tasks which are unique and not shared.

Rationale—The more the ratio between time in individual tasks and time in group tasks approaches 1.0, the greater is the possibility that a student learns to value both his or her individual and group responsibilities.

Assessment Procedure

1. *Tabulate* the amount of time devoted to individual tasks, that is, projects, reports, etc.

2. *Tabulate* the amount of time devoted to group tasks.

3. *Calculate* the ratio $\frac{\text{Time in individual tasks}}{\text{Time in group tasks}} = ?$

Sign XII: The teacher communicates clearly to children that learning is self-learning. Faith is demonstrated that all children want to become and pupils show satisfaction as they become aware of their growth.

Rationale—The greater the rate of quadric of ABCD sequences, the higher the possibility the student will learn that his or her learning is self-learning and experience joy in this learning.

Assessment Procedure

1. *Tabulate* the number of behaviors which follow the sequence (a) teacher asks either "what do you feel" or "what does that mean to you," (b) student expresses feeling and/or meaning, (c) teacher responds non-evaluatively to the student's statement, and (d) student shares more of the feeling or meaning.

2. *Construct* the ratio $\dfrac{\text{Number of ABCD sequences}}{\text{Time observed}} = ?$

Sign XIII: Evaluation is a shared process and includes more than academic achievement.

Rationale—The larger (numerically) the ratio, the greater the possibility that evaluation is a shared process and includes more than academic achievement. A corollary is that both of these factors increase the possibility that evaluation is a shared responsibility and that non-academic factors are also important.

Assessment Procedure

1. Ask the teacher (a) who is included in the students' evaluations and (b) what factors are included in student evaluation?

2. *Calculate* the ratio $\dfrac{\text{\% of evaluation by others}}{\text{\% of evaluation by teacher}} = ?$

3. *Calculate* the ratio $\dfrac{\text{Amount of evaluation for non-academic factors}}{\text{Amount of evaluation for academic factors}} = ?$

Sign XIV: Motivation for learning is high and seems inner-directed; pupil activity seems to say, "I've got a job I want to do."

Rationale—The larger (numerically) the ratio between the teacher's use of student initiated behaviors and the teacher's rejection or blockage of those behaviors, the higher the possibility that students are motivated to accomplish their own goals. It is felt that the students' initiation of questions and/or suggestions is a symptom of their being "turned on" by school. Additionally, the teacher's use of the students' behaviors is thought to be a stimulus for them.

Assessment Procedure

1. *Tabulate* the sequence of behaviors which follow the pattern (a) student asks question, (b) teacher answers question, and (c) student asks another question and/or comments on teacher's response.

2. *Tabulate* the sequence of behavior which follows the pattern (a) student makes suggestion for activity, (b) teacher accepts or extends the student's suggestion, and (c) the student responds to the teacher's response or makes a further suggestion for activity.

3. *Tabulate* the sequence of behaviors which follow the pattern (a) student asks question and (b) teacher ignores question or rejects it.

4. *Tabulate* the sequence of behaviors which follow the pattern (a) student makes suggestion for activity and (b) teacher ignores or rejects it.

5. *Calculate* the ratio $\frac{\text{Pattern 1} + \text{Pattern 2}}{\text{Pattern 3} + \text{Pattern 4}} = ?$

Processes and Products

The preceding discussion of the assessment of humane classrooms has presented some measurement procedures and ideas which may seem naive to some people who specialize in this area. On the other hand, they may appear somewhat "nit-picky" to educators who place little or no value on these indexes. This is the kind of balance we hoped to attain. We wanted to increase the usability of the criteria described in *Perceiving, Behaving, Becoming* for more rigorous investigation. Additionally, we hoped to "make sense" to those who want to determine the humaneness of their classrooms, but who are reluctant to get into a lot of complicated research procedures. We wanted to keep the procedures as straightforward as possible.

Some cornerstones for the success of such research efforts follow:

1. The investigations must explore the effects of humanism across extended periods of time of not less than one academic year.

2. The investigations must involve serious training of observers until they *attain* and *maintain* high levels of reliability (.85+).

3. Humanistic educators must conduct serious studies of the effects of the factors or variables they advocate. The emphasis is upon conducting our own research rather than depending on others to do it for us. This puts our destiny in our own hands.

4. Audio and video recordings of humane classroom procedures allow us to "freeze" a given interaction without losing its dynamic qualities.

These kinds of procedures work. They may appear non-rigorous to some assessment specialists, but the measures have a solid basis in successful research use. In a series of studies across 14 years, the National Consortium for Humanistic Education (NCHE) has used many of these procedures and variables to explore classroom behavior. They have clearly demonstrated that, through specific training procedures, it is possible to attain inter- and intra-rater reliabilities above .90 and to maintain them across a three year period.[4]

A second aspect of these variables and procedures is that they can be effective in predictive investigations as well as cause and effect studies. This means that on the one hand we are able to determine the level of variables in a given school context while on the other hand we can make fairly accurate predictions about student outcomes, such as academic achievement, I.Q. changes, absence rates, and discipline referrals. In cause and effect studies the NCHE found that teaching procedures which altered the levels of such variables also changed student outcomes.

A Sample of Results from Research on Humanistic Teaching

The National Consortium for Humanistic Education has carried out a series of impressive research studies under the leadership of David N. Aspy and Flora Roebuck. The results of these studies clearly affirm the usefulness of research techniques like those described earlier. They also provide significant support for the belief that humanistic practices not only make our schools more humane places for young people, they also contribute to the achievement of traditional goals like growth of intelligence and the acquisition of cognitive skills. The remainder of this section is adapted from Aspy and Roebuck's book, *A Lever Long Enough* and summarizes the findings of their early research.[5]

A Model. In spite of the lofty sound of it, a theoretical formulation is really just a model of what we see happening before us. As such it is only as valuable as it is accurate in helping us account for the events we observe. As one leader said, "Nothing is as practical as a good theory." Well, the studies that deal with human behavior do not have as many "good" theories as the physical sciences; that is, predictions based on theories of human behavior generally are less certain of becoming reality

[4] From: David N. Aspy and Flora Roebuck. *A Lever Long Enough.* Washington, D.C.: National Consortium for Humanistic Education, Catholic University, 1976. Reprinted by permission of the authors.

[5] *Ibid.*

than predictions based on theories from the physical sciences. It is therefore difficult to specify any behavioral theory. We have a large body of theoretical formulations, but virtually none of them can be called a theory. This means that we cope, as do other researchers in the behavioral sciences, with much uncertainty in the models undergirding or directing our investigations. Since we had both our philosophical commitment and the freedom to select among imperfect alternatives, we began our work by testing the formulations of Carl Rogers because they seemed to be the ones most consistent with our view of human behavior.

While Carl Rogers is most widely recognized for the founding of client-centered counseling, it may be that his most important contribution from a research point of view is his delineation of three factors which he thought were related to all human learning situations. Specifically, he contended that learning will be enhanced when the helper (teacher, counselor) provides high levels of empathy (E), congruence (C), and positive regard (PR). Fortunately these terms are fairly synonymous with more commonly used words, so we can say empathy = understanding, congruence = genuineness, and positive regard = valuing or respect. For our purposes, we could restate Rogers' formulations as "The higher the levels of understanding, genuineness, and respect a teacher gives to students, the more they will learn." This gave us a testable hypothesis which we explored in a series of studies described in the following sections. We have selected only pilot (prototypic) investigations from among the many conducted.

Levels of E, C, PR, and Cognitive Growth

To explore the relationship between Rogers' facilitative conditions and student learning, we studied the academic progress of 120 third grade students. By applying the Truax Scales for empathy, congruence, and positive regard to the classroom teaching performances of third grade teachers, we were able to identify three teachers who were providing high levels of facilitative conditions and three providing low levels of the same conditions. We then selected 60 students in the high conditions and matched them with 60 students in the low conditions. We controlled for sex, socioeconomic level, and I.Q. Pre- and post-testing of all of the students across one academic year indicated that those receiving high conditions made significantly (.01) more gains on their achievement test performance than those in low conditions. This supported Rogers' contention that the interpersonal facilitative conditions were significantly and positively related to cognitive growth. With the encouragement provided by the results of this first study, we pressed ahead.

Levels of E, C, PR, and I.Q.

The second question which emerged was whether or not the facilitative conditions were related to change in I.Q. as well as to differential achievement gains. This question was addressed with roughly the same procedure as the first. We identified first grade teachers' levels of interpersonal conditions, randomly selected 25 students in low conditions and matched them with a group of 25 students receiving high conditions. Results from pre- and post-testing across one academic year with the Stanford-Binet Intelligence Test indicated that those in high conditions made an average gain of nine points while those in low conditions made no significant change. Again, the evidence supported Rogers' formulations that interpersonal facilitation is positively and significantly related to I.Q. gains. We hypothesized that perhaps these gains were related to the students' ability to be more open to their experiences in a facilitative environment.

Levels of E, C, PR, and Student Attendance

In a continuing search for very basic data, we investigated the effect of levels of facilitation upon the most fundamental fact in school: attendance. This was a "rock bottom" measure in that students are either there or they're not. In the same manner as before, we assessed the teachers' levels of interpersonal functioning and compared the attendance rates of 60 third grade students in high conditions with a matched group of 60 in low conditions. The results showed that the average number of days students were absent in high conditions was significantly lower ($p \leq .05$) than in low conditions. That is, children missed fewer days of school when their teachers offered higher levels of the interpersonal facilitative conditions. Even in this very "hard core" dimension, Rogers' theorizing seemed to explain the events. Of course, this finding is consistent with common sense; most of us like to be in places where we are treated decently.

Teachers' Levels of E, C, and PR

As we studied students' levels of performance and their relationship to teachers' levels of interpersonal functioning, we built a store of information concerning the levels of interpersonal functioning throughout the teaching profession. Since the early evidence was from small studies, it was necessary to collect systematically some larger samples from a broader geographical distribution. This was accomplished by conducting a series of workshops for teachers throughout the country and collecting pre- and post-measures for the trainees. In this way we were able to get relatively large samples from Massachusetts, Maryland, Florida, Louisiana, Kansas, Kentucky, Michigan, North Carolina, Texas, and Minnesota.

Assessments of these samples indicated that geographical setting is not a significant source of variance in teachers' levels of interpersonal functioning; they indicated also that, as a group, elementary teachers are functioning slightly higher than secondary teachers. The general statement which seemed most justified by the data, however, was that most teachers were providing levels of interpersonal skills which tend to retard rather than facilitate learning by their students.

This finding was a challenge, rather than an indictment, because none of the professional groups (counselors included) were functioning any better. It seemed that most of us were in the same deteriorative network—one which served to keep all of us from developing to our fullest potential. In fact, our lack of effective interpersonal skills was crippling us before most of us even got started. Data from the broader society confirmed those being generated by our studies. For example, it is estimated that one person in ten will be hospitalized for insanity sometime in our lifetime, and that one in fourteen is an alcoholic.

Training Teachers for E, C, and PR

The foregoing seemed to describe a hopeless downhill spiral, but there was the possibility that systematic intervention (training) could increase teachers' levels of interpersonal skills. To assess this potentiality, we employed the Carkhuff procedures which had been developed for counselor training. The program involved a 15 hour didactic-experiential model of training with 5 hours of didactic instruction about the conditions for empathy, congruence, and positive regard; 5 hours of rating standard audio tape recordings of classroom instruction; and 5 hours of role-playing in groups to produce minimally facilitative levels of interpersonal conditions. This procedure was applied to three groups of elementary teachers (N = 200) and two groups of secondary teachers (N = 150) in two different settings. Pre- and post-training assessments revealed that the teachers entered at levels below minimally facilitative conditions, and during training, moved to facilitative levels. It appeared that teachers could be systematically trained to improve their levels of interpersonal functioning. Additional studies indicated that when teachers improved their interpersonal skills, the skills translated into the student gains found in the naturalistic studies. That is, teacher gain in interpersonal skills results in improved student performance.

The Sum of Research

In our preliminary investigations we had generated a data base which supported the following contentions:

1. Teachers' levels of Empathy, Congruence, and Positive Regard are positively and significantly related to the following:
   a. Students' cognitive growth
   b. Students' I.Q. gains
   c. Students' attendance

2. Teachers' levels of Empathy, Congruence, and Positive Regard are generally below those required for minimal facilitation of student growth.

3. Teachers' levels of Empathy, Congruence, and Positive Regard can be enhanced by systematic skills training as developed by Carkhuff.

4. Teachers' gains in levels of Empathy, Congruence, and Positive Regard are translated into positive growth by their students.

5. Geographical setting is not a significant cause of variability in levels of interpersonal functioning by teachers. In other words, the problem is national in scope.

6. The levels of interpersonal skills demonstrated by teachers are about the same as those of the general population. That is, the problem is cultural in nature.

As an indirect by-product of our work, we had generated a series of technologies by which it was possible (a) to diagnose levels of interpersonal skills, (b) to train for improvement of interpersonal skills, and (c) to assess the effects of the training in terms of both teacher behavior and student behaviors. Additionally, the training and feedback system could be applied to large populations as well as to individual teachers. Thus, we had developed in the area of interpersonal skills a technology that could be used for diagnosis, training, research, or any combination of the three activities.

PART III

A Checklist

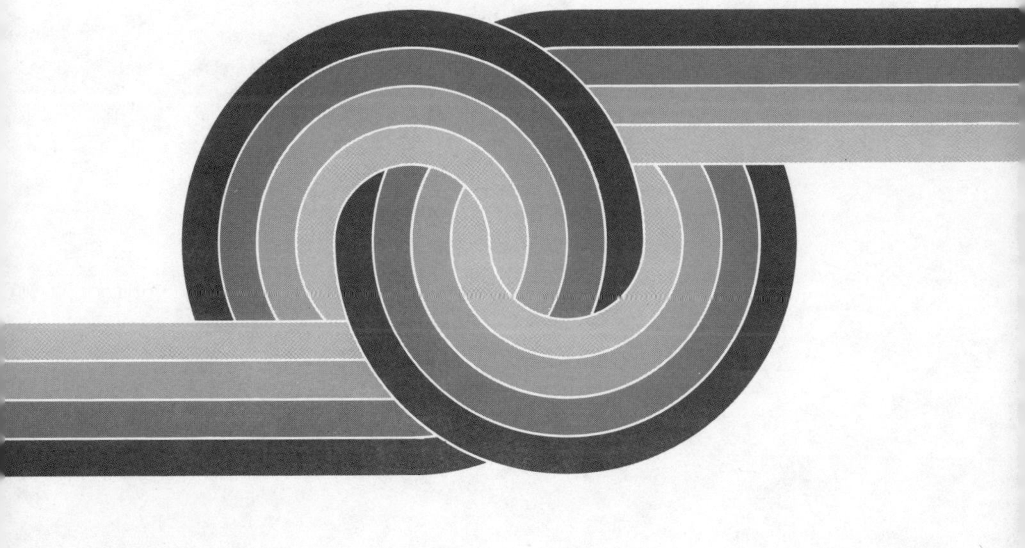

A Checklist for Humanistic Schools

Doris M. Brown

Purpose of the Checklist

If the renewed effort toward humanism in the schools is to take hold, theory and research related to the field must be made available to teachers. Above all, it must be understandable. Teachers and others who deal directly with students need to know what is really meant by humanistic education. Professional texts, program guides, and simulation activities for the classroom are used to move toward affective ends, but few sources are available which specify a variety of probable indicators of the "humanistic condition."

One responsibility of the checklist task force of the ASCD Working Group on Humanistic Education was to devise a checklist for assessing the humanistic orientation of a local school or classroom. The checklist is intended to be useful in:

1. Observing the degree to which school systems, schools, teachers, and students are operating in humanistic ways.

2. Getting teachers, administrators, and other school personnel to examine their own practices, then setting and pursuing goals for improving them.

3. Helping parents, board members, legislators, and the general public better understand and support humanistic endeavors of schools.

Although not a complete instrument, the checklist provides, (a) a starting point which school practitioners may use for exploring current practice, and (b) a list of humanistic conditions that may serve schools and teachers as a reference source for designing humanistic practices. The list can be used in its present form, or as a model for locally produced instruments.

How the Checklist Was Developed

Our work began with a series of discussions which probed into the meaning of humanistic education and practice. Working as a group and in teams of two we tried to write brief, concise humanistic practices which are observable or can be simply assessed by inference or a question or two. We edited each other's work. If we missed a favored item which one team had thrown out, we presented our case for reinstating it when we met again as a group. We consulted the literature, as well as publications from school districts, professional organizations, and universities. We diligently translated each to more precise wording. We talked with individuals and groups who worked in humanistic ways. Through this exploring and winnowing process a consensus was reached on a starting list of 125 items.

We next had the list examined by 205 elementary and secondary educators asking them to rate each item as very useful, useful, or not useful as an indicator of humanism in schools. We also asked them to edit our work and suggest additions they considered useful or necessary.

Next step was to present the refined list of 100 descriptors to the ASCD open meetings of the Working Group on Humanistic Education at Miami Beach in March 1976. Forty-six ASCD members worked with the checklist committee. They (a) rated the items on a five-point scale, (b) suggested new items and the rewording of others, and (c) suggested ways of field testing. After the meeting, all items rated in the two lowest categories by six or more of our ASCD participants were dropped. New items suggested by the Miami group or extracted from study of additional material sent by individuals following the conference resulted in the printing of a revised checklist of 125 items.

The revised checklist was finally rated by a random sample of 241 teachers, administrators, and high school students who indicated on a five-point scale the importance of the 125 items. The 241 raters represented five groups. There were 28 ASCD Affective Education Institute participants, 44 elementary teachers, 44 administrators, 69 teacher trainees, and 56 secondary students. There was agreement by all five groups on the importance of the items. Mean ratings of each item by all groups were not lower than the "Somewhat Important" middle category, and only seven ranked in that category. Although there was general agreement on the importance of items, there was little agreement among groups on the degree of importance of individual items. Highest raters were the ASCD members who attended the December 1976 Affective Education Institute and the March 1976 open session of the Working Group on Humanistic Education. Lowest raters were the secondary school students. As a consequence of this final rating, the 25 lowest rated items were dropped resulting in a Checklist of 100 rank ordered items. The final form of the Checklist for Humanistic Schools is presented at the end of this report, pages 52-55.

The Scoring, Content, and Field-Testing of the Checklist

Scoring the Checklist. The Checklist for Humanistic Schools is purposely presented without an established scoring procedure. The committee believes the kinds of uses suggested in the Field Test section following are far more significant applications of the Checklist than reduction of the content to numerical scores. Users of the Checklist are, therefore, free to devise whatever scoring system best meets their needs, purposes, and local conditions. Some persons who have used the Checklist have experimented with two scoring categories, *Yes* or *No;* three categories, *Much, Some,* or *Little;* or a five point scale from *Much* to *None.*

Content of the Checklist. An analysis of the 100 statements in the Checklist reveals that 40 percent deal with teacher attitudes and actions which free learners to think independently and select what they are interested in and want to learn. Actual learning activities are represented in about 19 percent of the items. These can be described as being experiential, creative, open, challenging, spontaneous, and personalized. Some take the students into the community to explore careers and to be of service to others. Sixteen percent have to do with student interaction with other students; for example, sharing, assisting, listening, and taking some responsibility for setting and following school and classroom procedures. Materials and facilities considerations account for 13 percent of the statements. Most of these refer to variety, easy access by students, and freedom of use. The remaining 12 percent are concerned that other persons in the school setting such as principals, parents, and community members contribute to the instructional program and receive benefits themselves from interacting with students and staff.

In summary, most items related to teacher and peer behaviors, such as listening, understanding, and helping. They also involve independence in learning and behaviors which would appear to exist as a result of what has been described as entering, understanding, and expanding the perceptual field.

Humanistic Objectives in the Checklist. The checklist items have also been scrutinized for compatibility with the goals and objectives of humanistic education as described earlier. The list is found to stand the test well. Evidence is briefly reviewed below with two checklist items selected to demonstrate each goal. Checklist number is in parenthesis.

Goal 1: Priority Given to Learner's Needs

Developmental characteristics considered more than age and grade when planning. (15)

Learning organized around student's own problem or question. (49)

Goal 2: Facilitates Self-Actualization

Students readily assisting and sharing with other students. (22)

Students able to go to the school resource center whenever needed. (96)

Goal 3: Fosters Acquisition of Skills for a Multicultural Society

Curriculum materials accurately reflecting our multiethnic society and varying family structures. (28)

Staff seeking training in communications and human relations. (37)

Goal 4: Personalizes Decisions and Practices

Wide variety of courses and special events from which to choose. (36)

Staff able to detect and respond appropriately to signs of personal problems of students. (16)

Goal 5: Utilizes Personal Values and Perceptions

Principal using the staff and students in making decisions affecting them. (9)

Teacher not expecting students to come up with answers he/she has in mind. (86)

Goal 6: Develops Environment Which Nurtures Growth

Activities encouraging divergent thinking and other creative effort. (12)

Free access to counselors, nurses, tutors, and other special personnel. (17)

Goal 7: Develops Concerns for Worth of Others

Planned interactions which foster appreciation of human differences. (39)

Evaluation of student work emphasizing correct responses instead of errors. (38)

The fact that there are few items about acquiring knowledge is not meant to imply that the cognitive area is not important. Knowing, in fact, is what the humanistic effort is all about. Being knowledgeable is one characteristic of humaneness, along with openness to experience, positive view of self, and oneness with others (Combs, *Perceiving, Behaving, Becoming,* 1962). Humanism is not anti-intellectual. Quite the contrary. The humanistic position is that students will learn *anything* better when schools and teachers are concerned with the human nature and function of students. Cognitive learning is far more likely to occur in an atmosphere where warm human relations nurture acquisition of knowledge and skill.

The instrument presents indicators of "what are" rather than "what should be" humane school practices. The items are not derived from empirical research which might have revealed even more behaviors indicative of humane or empathic considerations. Such research is not plentiful nor is it usually in a form that can readily be translated into a range of specific organizational and human practices. The items represent those observations that a sample of educators and students believe are indicative of school situations conducive to learning and, at the very least, are pleasant places in which to engage in learning activities.

Having come at this instrument development task from practices and beliefs rather than from a base of research, it is encouraging to find empirical and theoretical research (in the previous section of this report) that seems to support what educators and students say are some of the practices that make learning more pleasant, exciting, and effective. Still, it is a difficult job to pick out behaviors that tell us the school is humanistic. In fact, it is often impossible to do so. What is a humane or considerate action toward one child can be inhumane and inconsiderate when taken toward another. Each has his or her own perceptual world. Humanism includes recognizing that individual perceptions exist and that perceptions vary with the time, place, and situation. This is why we encourage readers to adapt use of the checklist to their own local needs.

An Alternative Organization of the Checklist. The checklist presented on pages 52-55 is organized with items in rank order beginning with those indicated in our development testing as most significant indicators of humanistic schools to those less so at the end. Users may wish to organize the checklist for their own purposes into various areas. Items could be arranged in several areas in order to highlight particular aspects of practice. For example, items might be organized into five areas such as the following:

Teacher-Student Interactions—Sample Items:

Teachers who are genuine, warm, and empathic.

Staff treating students with same courtesy and respect accorded peers.

Adults laughing with students.

Teachers making verbal or nonverbal responses to students to indicate, "I hear you."

Student Activities—Sample Items:

Students involved in discovery and "hands on" activities.

Free discussion of questions and issues not covered in the text.

Students questioning accuracy, applicability, and appropriateness of information.

Students involved in career exploration through out-of-school assignments.

Student-Student Interactions—Sample Items:

Students listening to each other.

Students readily assisting and sharing with other students.

Class meetings held to discuss solutions to problems which arise.

Materials and Facilities—Sample Items:

A resource center in which students are free to use projectors, filmstrip viewers, and cassette recorders.

Student access to materials for on-going projects.

Other Persons in School—Sample Items:

Parents welcomed as members of the instructional team.

Principals and teachers seeking suggestions from parents.

Field Tested Uses of the Checklist for Humanistic Schools

1. *General Awareness*

The humanistic thrust in the schools should be understood by parents, the general community, and others not in education but influencing decisions about schools. When developing plans for accountability and skill mastery by students, human relations skills must not be overlooked. Citizen groups need to know the meaning of humanistic education and how it accelerates student academic achievement.

Parent groups and boards of education have used the Checklist as source material in discussing aspirations and projecting outcomes for newly integrated schools.

2. *Goal Congruence*

Administrators, students, support personnel, and community members can use the instrument for making decisions about goals toward which they need to be working cooperatively.

The list was used by several staffs in the preschool opening sessions to agree upon and establish priorities for humanistic goals for the new year.

3. *Self-Evaluation*

Individual teachers can use the checklist to determine which practices they feel are critical and to assess the extent to which such critical activities are taking place in their classrooms. Once this has been done individually and in small teams, the teacher can better decide on which specifics of humanism he or she wants to improve.

Several staffs used this procedure as the initial step in the teacher evaluation process.

4. *Staff Development Goals*

Self-evaluation results can be vital to in-service education program goals. The data collected will not only indicate which behaviors teachers most want to improve but will also indicate how in-service programs can be structured.

In field-tested uses, some districtwide needs were met by repeating a well designed program in all schools. Other less universal needs have been met by offering a variety of humanistic growth programs through a teacher center. Needs unique to a few individuals were met by on-the-job programs and programs of self-study.

5. *In-service Training in Human Skills*

Once the objectives and structure of a teacher improvement program have been set, content and procedure can be selected. Programs which focus on qualities like empathy, congruence, and positive regard for others and which are led by persons already possessing those characteristics are especially useful. These same characteristics can be sought in all of a school's Human Skills in-service component and in technical and content components as well.

6. *Program Evaluation*

The checklist can be and has been used for pre- and post-testing of the effectiveness of in-service training. The testing is at the teacher perception level, but could equally well be used through observation. The list has also been used to assess teacher perception of the effectiveness of humanistic classroom practices and for implementing humanistic goals of a special Title VII school desegregation project.

7. *Maintenance of Effort*

A rather special use of the checklist is for keeping high visibility on the humanistic effort. Selected items can be included as a regular section in district-community publications. Classroom photos can be used for greater impact. Achivement score summaries and humanistic achievement honors can give balance and credence.

During the field-testing, five items from the checklist were included in each issue of a local education newsletter. Teaching teams were also asked to evaluate themselves and set new targets.

8. *Developing Curriculum*

A list of humanistic school practices is a natural source for deriving affective objectives in constructing new or revised curricula.

Several district curriculum development groups used the items for this purpose. It was also used in a graduate teacher education course in curriculum construction. An exercise in blending process and traditional subjects helps teachers see both the ease and desirability of building affective objectives and experiences into even the most traditional of the content areas.

Those of us on the ASCD working group who developed the Checklist for Humanistic Schools found the task both challenging and rewarding. We have a better understanding of the relationship between humanistic values and learning and feel we are better teachers as a result. We hope you share our enthusiasm for the checklist and will be able to use it in your classroom and schools. We know you will find putting humanistic teaching into practice an enriching experience for you as well as for your students.

Checklist for Humanistic Schools*

Items are listed in rank order as arranged by Educators, Teachers, and High School Students.

1. Teachers who are genuine, warm, and empathic.
2. Student mistakes not resulting in a damaged self-concept.
3. Policies aimed directly at maintaining personal worth, dignity, and rights of students.
4. Staff treating students with same courtesy and respect accorded peers.
5. Students listening to each other.
6. Necessary disciplinary treatment tempered with compassion and understanding.
7. Staff emphasizing positive rather than negative consequences in guiding behavior.

* Members of the Checklist for Humanistic Schools Task Force were: Doris M. Brown, Task Force Chairperson; Sarah Caldwell, Shirley King, George Pressey, and Shirley Salmon.

8. A library with an abundance of books and other materials.

9. Principal truly using the staff and students in making decisions which affect them.

10. Teachers conveying through action that they trust the students.

11. At least once a day, teachers finding the time and incident to indicate to each student "I care who you are."

12. Activities which encourage divergent thinking and other forms of creative effort.

13. Teachers using objectives for humane teaching rather than against it; student choice, pacing; teacher time management for greater individual attention.

14. Teachers showing competence in subject matter content.

15. Developmental characteristics of students taken into consideration more than age and grade when planning learning experiences.

16. Staff able to detect and respond appropriately to signs of personal problems of students.

17. Free access to counselors, nurses, tutors, and other special personnel.

18. Teachers making verbal or nonverbal responses to students to indicate "I hear you."

19. All students receive some "ego-builders," honors status, roles, "happy grams," positive comments by others.

20. Teachers giving observations as feedback, not judgment.

21. Small group field trips and excursions which make in-school learning relevant.

22. Students readily assisting and sharing with other students.

23. Students involved in discovery and "hands on" activities.

24. A school philosophy, including values and attitude concerns, being used by teachers in planning classroom activities.

25. Free discussion of questions and issues not covered in the text.

26. Teachers motivating students with intrinsic value of ideas or activity.

27. Teachers having greater concern for the person involved than for task achievement.

28. Curriculum materials accurately reflecting our multiethnic society and varying family structures.

29. Evidence of well-planned lessons.

30. Access to activities regardless of sex, age, personality, and other characteristics.

31. Interest or learning centers being used with purpose.

32. Students talking enthusiastically about what they are doing in school.

33. Teachers making comments during a dialogue with students: for example, "tell me more," "that sounds interesting."

34. New students and family members given a tour of the building and an explanation of the program.

35. A student attitude of, "I've chosen this hard thing. Learning is challenging, stretching, sometimes hard, but oh so worth it!"

36. Wide variety of courses and special events from which to choose.

37. Staff seeking training in communications and human relations.

38. Evaluation of student work emphasizing correct responses instead of errors.

39. Planned school interactions which foster appreciation of human differences.

40. Students questioning accuracy, applicability, and appropriateness of information.

41. Spontaneous discussions being encouraged.

42. Principals and teachers seeking suggestions from parents.

43. An entrance area with a friendly decor which displays students' work.

44. Students involved in self-evaluation.

45. Students, teachers, and parents displaying symbols of school pride.

46. Students sharing classroom and school responsibilities.

47. Teachers knowing specific things each student likes and dislikes, as well as personal tragedies and successes.

48. Adults laughing with students; lots of smiling.

49. Learning organized around students' own problems or questioning.

50. Community volunteers assisting in learning centers, libraries, teaching technical skills, and serving as special resources.

51. Opportunities for students to be involved in career exploration or job location through out-of-school work.

52. A resource center in which students are free to use projectors, filmstrip viewers, and cassette tape recorders.

53. Teachers who view teaching as "freeing" rather than controlling.

54. Class meetings held to discuss solutions to problems which arise.

55. Space outside where people can run.

56. Teachers seeking parents' evaluation of child's progress.

57. Student records which note student's strengths and interests more than limitations.

58. Playground with grass as well as asphalt.

59. Teacher stopping to talk to parents in the school.

60. Teachers questioning misconceptions, faulty logic, and unwarranted conclusions.

61. Teachers working, playing, learning along with the students.

62. Evaluations as important in areas of personal-social development as in academic progress.

63. Spontaneous laughter.

64. Representative student governments dealing with relevant school problems.

65. Utilization of available non-classroom space for activities, learning centers, tutoring.

66. Teachers building student ideas into the curriculum.

67. Teacher disclosing aspects of own experience relevant to the teaching-learning.

68. System for students accepting responsibility for movement within the school, and to other places of learning.

69. Outsiders feeling welcome in the classroom.

70. Classes working outdoors when it is appropriate to the experience.

71. Student access to materials for on-going projects.

72. Principal spending some of his or her time working with students.

73. Space to "move around" in every classroom.

74. Availability of tools and scientific instruments for use by the students.

75. Staff and students sharing resources.

76. Student sub-groupings based on special interests, social preference, as well as skill needs.

77. Parents welcomed as a member of instructional team.

78. Classwork evolving from out-of-school events in the lives of students.

79. A brief period each day to do "fun things."

80. Teacher talk supplemented with some friendly physical gestures.

81. Presence of alternatives to traditional grading systems.

82. "I'll help with that" actions by teachers.

83. Students working independently on what concerns them.

84. Secretary providing a positive greeting when meeting visitors, students, and faculty.

85. Presence of human development and study of humankind as a regular part of the curriculum.

86. Teacher not always expecting students to come up with answer he or she has in mind.

87. An absence of negative comments to students by teachers.

88. Students working independently in small groups.

89. Teachers greeting students entering and leaving classroom.

90. A setting for student dramatic and musical productions.

91. Students having time to sit, think, and mull things over.

92. All students evaluating the classroom and school instructional program.

93. Senior citizens involved with students, at school, in their homes, and in care homes.

94. Students doing some of the teaching and other leadership tasks.

95. Student task-oriented committees.

96. Students able to go to the school resource center whenever needed.

97. Teachers spending some of their unscheduled time with students.

98. Libraries, laboratories, shops, and recreational areas available to students after school hours.

99. Surprise exhibits such as a litter of pups, white rabbits, unusual type plants.

100. Students engaged in community service.

Contributors to This Booklet

Arthur W. Combs, Chairperson; Distinguished Professor, University of Northern Colorado, Greeley

David N. Aspy, College of Applied Health, Eastern Kentucky University, Richmond

Doris M. Brown, School of Education, University of Missouri, St. Louis

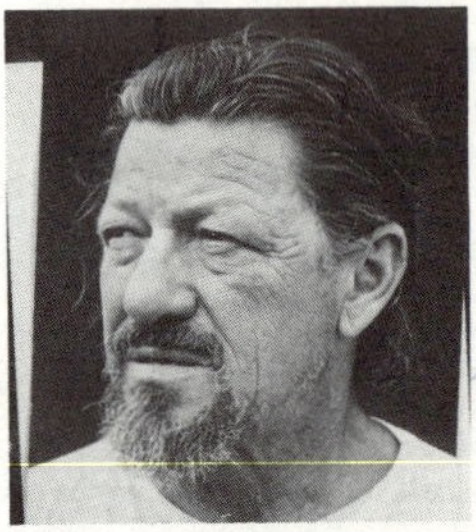

Morrel J. Clute, Division of Educational Leadership, Wayne State University, Detroit

Laurabeth H. Hicks, Bureau of Occupational and Adult Education, U.S. Office of Education, Washington, D.C.

Elizabeth S. Randolph, Assistant Superintendent, Charlotte-Mecklenburg Schools, North Carolina